RACE CAR LEGENDS

The Allisons
Mario Andretti
Crashes & Collisions
Demolition Derby
Drag Racing
Dale Earnhardt
Famous Finishes
Formula One Racing
A. J. Foyt
Jeff Gordon
History of NASCAR
Kenny Irwin Jr.
The Jarretts
The Labonte Brothers
The Making of a Race Car
Mark Martin
Jeremy Mayfield
Monster Trucks & Tractors
Motorcycles
Richard Petty
The Pit Crew
Stunt Driving
The Unsers
Rusty Wallace
Women in Racing

CHELSEA HOUSE PUBLISHERS

MARK MARTIN

Tara Baukus Mello

CHELSEA HOUSE PUBLISHERS
Philadelphia

Frontis photo: *Mark Martin is all smiles as he waves to the fans from victory lane after winning the Goodwrench Service 200 in 1996.*

Produced by
21st Century Publishing and Communications, Inc.
New York, New York
http://www.21cpc.com

CHELSEA HOUSE PUBLISHERS

Editor in Chief: Stephen Reginald
Managing Editor: James D. Gallagher
Production Manager: Pamela Loos
Art Director: Sara Davis
Director of Photography: Judy L. Hasday
Senior Production Editor: LeeAnne Gelletly
Publishing Coordinator: James McAvoy
Assistant Editor: Anne Hill
Cover Illustration & Design: Keith Trego

Front Cover Photo: AP/Wide World Photos
Back Cover Photos: AP Photos/Chuck Burton & AP Photos/Alan Marler

The Chelsea House World Wide Website address is
http://www.chelseahouse.com

First Printing

1 3 5 7 9 8 6 4 2

Library of Congress Cataloging-in-Publication Data

Mello, Tara Baukus.
   Mark Martin / Tara Baukus Mello.
   64 p.   cm.—(Race car legends)
   Includes bibliographical references and index.
   Summary: A biography of the automobile racer who in 1998 became the first driver to win four International Race of Champions titles.
   ISBN 0-7910-5411-X
   1. Martin, Mark, 1959–   —Juvenile literature. 2. Automobile racing drivers—United States—Biography—Juvenile literature. [1. Martin, Mark, 1959–   . 2. Automobile racing drivers.] I. Title. II. Series.
GV1032.M36M45 1999
796.72'092—dc21
[B]   99-15640
                                                               CIP
                                                                AC

CONTENTS

CHASING THE CHAMPIONSHIP

It was a hot Saturday night in Bristol, Tennessee, when Mark Martin and the rest of the Winston Cup drivers began the Goody's Headache Powders 500. Like every other driver on the field, Mark wanted to win this race, to get the prize money and capture some of the coveted points that determine who will be the Winston Cup champion at the end of the season.

The desire to win was even stronger for Mark. He was second in points for the season, just 92 points behind leader Jeff Gordon. Jeff had won the last four races, tying the record for the most races won in a row. If Jeff won this race, he would break the record. Since 1989, Mark had been among the top six drivers in the point totals at the end of each season. Yet Mark had never won a Winston Cup championship. He was hoping that 1998 would be his year, and winning this race would put him one step closer.

Mark Martin celebrates his victory at the Goody's 500 at Bristol Motor Speedway, Tennessee, on August 22, 1998.

Pallbearers at the funeral of Mark Martin's father, who was killed in a plane crash only two weeks before Mark won the Goody's 500.

Winning the Goody's Headache Powders 500 was even more important to Mark than the other races that year. Just a couple of weeks earlier, Mark's father, Julian, his stepmother, Shelley, and stepsister, Sarah, had been killed in a plane crash. When Mark entered the Pepsi 400 the weekend after they died, he hoped to win and dedicate his victory to his family. Although Mark led for part of the race, he lost the lead when Jeff Gordon charged past him as soon as the race restarted after a caution flag. When it was over, Mark placed fourth.

So on Saturday, August 22, 1998, Mark Martin climbed in his Valvoline/Cummins Ford Taurus with winning heavy on his mind. Starting in fourth position, he was finally able to capture the lead on lap 191 when he snuck by Jeremy Mayfield. Mark stayed in the lead for just nine laps before he lost it to Dale Jarrett, who was first out of the pits during a caution period.

The track at the Bristol Motor Speedway is known as "the world's fastest half-mile," and cars that race on it frequently run very close together. The track, which is a .533-mile oval, has steep, 36-degree banked concrete turns. As a result, cars often get a little too close, causing the caution flag to come out. During this race, the caution flag appeared 13 times, for a total of 86 laps.

As the race continued, Mark stayed in the top five positions on the track, but he did not get back in the lead until lap 320, when he was able to get by Bobby Labonte on the outside. Just 15 laps later, Mark had a close call when rookie driver Jerry Nadeau spun in front of him. Reacting quickly, Mark was able to go low on the track and drove through the smoke without a scratch.

It was not long, however, before Mark had another close call when Darrell Waltrip bumped him in the side. Fortunately Mark was able to maintain his lead position and win the race, crossing the finish line 2.185 seconds ahead of his teammate Jeff Burton.

"I was right at the start/finish line when [the bump] happened," said Mark. "I didn't have a chance to analyze the whole situation. . . . That could have cost me the win, and it made me pretty mad."

Weary from the long hot race on the difficult Bristol track, Mark said, "I cried last week because I didn't get to dedicate a win to my dad and Shelley and Sarah. This was for them. He would have been proud of this one tonight."

Although he had been devastated over the death of his father, stepmother, and stepsister, Mark would go on with his career without missing a single race. Mark knew that his father, who got him involved in racing, wouldn't want him to miss a race, which would mean risking the championship that Mark worked hard toward every race season.

With the win at the Goody's 500, Mark was now one step closer to the Winston Cup championship. With 12 races left in the season, he was just 67 points behind the leader Jeff Gordon, but Mark knew that winning the championship wouldn't be easy. Jeff Gordon, his crew chief Ray Evernham, and the entire Rainbow Warrior team were a hard bunch to beat.

Mark was giving each race his best effort. At the end of July, he had become the first driver to win four International Race of Champions (IROC) titles. In the IROC series, drivers from different types of racing compete in identically prepared cars. In 1998, the drivers, including Jeff Gordon, Al Unser Jr., Tom Kendall, and Tony Stewart, all raced Pontiac Trans Am Firebirds.

In the 40-lap IROC race, Mark was in last place, 12th, as he slowly began to work his way up. On the 37th lap, he passed Jimmy Vasser, who had been leading from the first lap. Al

Unser Jr. fought hard to take over the lead, but Mark won the race by about a quarter of a second, also winning the series. "This is truly the highlight of my career. This is it. This is the best," Mark said enthusiastically.

Winning the Goody's 500 at Bristol was a small step toward helping Mark get over the death of his loved ones, but he still needed to work hard to have a chance at the championship. He said, "I want to win this championship

The crowd cheers them on as the rivalry between Jeff Gordon and Mark Martin (in two front cars) continues at the Sam's Town 300 in Las Vegas, March 6, 1999. Martin, who had won the pole position, also won the race.

pretty darn bad, and I really want to be a successful Winston Cup driver. What that means is winning races and being a contender."

Mark did not miss a single race that he had scheduled for the year, including 15 Busch Grand National races and 33 Winston Cup races. On Labor Day weekend, Mark first raced 200 miles in his Winn-Dixie Ford in a Busch Grand National race. The next day he climbed into his Winston Cup car to compete in the Pepsi Southern 500 in Darlington, South Carolina. After driving 500 miles in his Valvoline Ford, Mark flew across the country to California. In Los Angeles, he drove the Valvoline/Hot Wheels Ford NASCAR Featherlite Southwest Tour car in the Ford L.A. Street Race, which is on a 1.4-mile course in the streets of Los Angeles.

Competing in three races in one weekend was grueling, but Mark was prepared. He said, "If you eat right, get plenty of rest, exercise, and take care of yourself on a regular basis, a trip like this is not quite as bad."

As the 1998 season continued, the gap between Jeff Gordon and Mark grew wider, even though Mark continued to race well. At the MBNA Gold 400 in Dover, Delaware, Mark not only won the race but also led for an incredible 380 of 400 laps. Even with the win, Mark was now 194 points behind Jeff. There were seven races left in the season, and it was still possible for Mark to make up the difference and win the championship. But everyone, including Mark, knew how strong Jeff's team was.

Two races later, victory was Mark's again, this time at the Charlotte Motor Speedway. Still, he was 174 points behind Jeff. Mark knew the next two races would be hard to win. Both required the use of engines with restrictor-plates, a plate between the intake manifold and the carburetor, which reduces the horsepower of the engine. The team simply was not very strong at restrictor-plate racing. During the first of the two races, Mark was involved in a multi-car accident and ended up placing 34th. At that point, the team knew that their chances at the 1998 championship were slim.

Mark placed second, third, and fourth at the last three races of the season, however, he was never able to catch Jeff Gordon and at the end of the season finished second in the point standings. Although he did not win the championship, Mark was still happy with his year. He said, "This is the greatest year of my life. I don't see how anybody could look at this year and think it was a failure."

THE DRIVE
TO RACE

Mark Martin was born on January 9, 1959, to Julian and Jackie Martin. He and his big sister, Glenda, lived with their parents in Batesville, Arkansas. Mark's father, Julian, owned a trucking company and his mother, Jackie, helped manage the business.

Growing up, Mark had many hobbies. He cared for tropical fish and also liked ceramics, making items such as drinking mugs, which he gave to family members. One of Mark's favorite hobbies was baseball. He played Little League and quickly realized that he had a knack for stealing bases.

The fascination with moving vehicles started early for Mark. His first mode of transportation was a bicycle, which he rode as often as he could, sometimes 10 miles a day after school. Mark said, "I don't remember how many miles I ever got on it, but I wore bikes out. Most people make bikes last forever. I wore them out."

Mark Martin and his son Matt after Mark's win at the Dura-Lube 200 at Darlington Raceway in March, 1996. Matt, like his father, is taking an early interest in car racing.

By age eight, the desire to go faster had kicked in. Mark wanted a minibike or a go-kart. Mark's parents made him wait until he was older, but they did start teaching him to "drive" while he was still quite young. Mark would steer from his father's lap while his dad operated the foot pedals and directed him. Although Mark was young to be learning driving skills, this played an important role in his future in racing.

By 1971 his father's trucking company had a fleet of refrigerated trucks, and one was actually owned by Mark. With $1,000 that he had saved, 12-year-old Mark took over the payments on an 18-wheel semi-truck, which he leased to his father's business. Although Mark did not even have his driver's license, he was very proud of his vehicle. He washed it himself and helped perform the regular maintenance on it.

Soon Mark had his first motorcycle and very quickly became addicted to speed. The local police pulled him over more than once. Mark's motorcycle-riding days ended when he hit a car in an intersection. By coincidence, Mark's dad was in an accident with his motorcycle about the same time as Mark and the two Martins ended up in the same hospital. Mark's accident was pretty serious, and his parents decided that it was too dangerous for him to continue riding a motorcycle.

A few years later, Mark got his first taste of racing. It was the summer of 1973, and Mark's dad, Julian, had taken him to the National Association for Stock Car Auto Racing (NASCAR) races at Daytona and Talladega. Julian loved stock car racing and even gave

some financial support to a local racer. That summer Mark worked in the pits, pulling the mud from the car after it was done competing on the dirt track in Locust Grove, Arkansas. It was then that Mark started asking his father to build him a race car. He was a freshman in high school.

It took Mark a while to get his father to consent to building him a car, but Julian finally agreed at the end of 1973. Mark's mom, Jackie,

Mark Martin loved riding his motorcycle at high speeds until an accident convinced his parents that he should give it up.

At age 15, Mark Martin began racing regularly at local tracks. He became known as the "teen-aged racing sensation."

was very concerned about her son's safety, but the pair assured her that they were taking lots of safety precautions. Eventually they convinced her, and she supported the project. Mark and Julian worked all winter on a 1955 Chevrolet with Julian's cousin Troy Lynn Jeffrey and an auto shop owner named Larry Shaw.

By spring they had finished their work on the car. It was painted bright orange and had a roll cage that Julian built himself. It was one of the many things Mark's dad did to make sure he was safe. "It was a pretty heavy car because I put so much bracing in it. He was my little boy and I was scared of him getting hurt. We seated Mark in the center of the car, way back towards the back. I didn't want to get him killed and I figured that was the safest place for him," said Julian.

They had been working on the car for many months now and Mark was anxious to get out on the track. He had driven a few practice laps the year before and was ready to compete. When they arrived at the Locust Grove track on April 12, 1974, the team caught everyone's attention. The shiny new race car with its perfect bodywork stood out from most of the other local racers. Plus there was a kid driving. Mark was small for a 15 year-old. He weighed a little more than 100 pounds and was about five feet tall. Getting Mark registered as a competitor was not easy either. Not only was he not old enough to drive, he was not even old enough to be in the pits! His parents had to sign special papers so he could race.

When Mark's first race began, he got off to a good start. He was doing well until he hit a pothole in the dirt a few laps into the race. Without a fence to keep him on the track, Mark spun out of control and slid over the bank of the first turn. Mark found himself in the same situation as many drivers before him. It almost always meant the end of the race for the driver, but not for Mark. His home-built six-cylinder engine kept going strong, and Mark drove through the weeds to a road by the track. Near the third turn, Mark drove his Chevy back on to the track and joined the race again. At the end of the day, he had finished sixth.

Mark began racing regularly and soon was

known as the "teen-aged racing sensation."
The people who owned the tracks in the area
promoted Mark, and race fans would come
just to see what this "kid" could do. From the
start it was clear that Mark had talent and by
the middle of his first racing season, he had a
shelf full of trophies at home to prove it. But
just because the team was running well did
not mean that it was easy.

Julian sponsored driver Wayne Brooks in an
effort to find out more about the process of
building a race car. He and the rest of the crew
went to Wayne's shop night after night to learn
how to build a race engine. On the track,
Wayne encouraged Mark to follow him as a way
to learn by doing. Although it was a lot of hard
work, the team was determined to learn everything they could as quickly as possible so they
could be competitive.

The team learned some of its lessons the
hard way. In June Mark competed at the Ben-
ton Speedbowl in his first long race. Well into
the race he was leading the pack of cars when,
all of a sudden, the car stopped running. It
had run out of gas. Mark was upset with his
crew for the mistake and told them they needed
to do better or they were going to have to find
another driver. As an adult, Mark looked back
on this incident and said, "They didn't laugh at
the time, but they sure thought that was funny
for some stupid kid to be tellin' them that. But
I was pretty much a driver by then."

Even in the beginning of his career, Mark
had the natural skills to be a successful driver.
He could feel the slightest changes that the
crew had made in tuning his car. He also knew
how to explain how the car was acting on the

*Mark Martin talks with his crew chief Jimmy Fennig at the Watkins Glen,
N.Y., race track in 1998. Martin's ability to explain how his car acts on the
track adds to his success as a race driver.*

track, so the crew could make further adjustments. This is one of the talents that makes Mark a successful driver today.

It was September of 1974 and Mark won the Arkansas Six-Cylinder Championship. After competing in well over 100 races, Mark was no longer a rookie on the dirt tracks, but he still had things to learn. The winter before the 1975 racing season was devoted to building a car for Mark that had some new features. It had a lighter-weight, yet stronger roll cage, an adjustable rear suspension, and a lower front end. The driver's seat was also moved from the center to the left side of car.

Mark raced well in 1975 and many other drivers began to dislike the team. They were bothered by the fact that someone so young and inexperienced was outracing them most of the time. According to the journal Mark kept about his racing, he won 51 out of 96 races, finishing second 32 times.

In 1976 Mark and the team decided to move up from a six-cylinder engine to the V-8 engine class for stock cars. Mark's new car was almost three times more powerful than the car he had driven the year before. He had trouble racing until the crew added power steering, which helped Mark keep the car under control. After a few races, things got better and Mark was once again a solid competitor.

Toward the end of the season, Mark raced on an asphalt track for the first time. The track was in Springfield, Missouri, the territory of a driver named Larry Phillips. Often Larry raced against big-name drivers who were hired by the track as a promotion to get more people to come to the races. Donnie Allison, one of the top NASCAR Winston Cup drivers at that time, was hired for the night Mark raced.

Mark held his own against Larry and Donnie. Larry led for most of the race, with Donnie close behind and Mark in third. Mark struggled to keep up, pushing the car to go faster and faster, until his engine blew midway through the race. Despite the fact that he could not finish the race, the crowd gave him a standing ovation for his performance. Mark's popularity as a driver was continuing to grow, and two of the Martins' friends started a Mark Martin Fan Club. Later that year Mark won the "Driver of the Year" contest sponsored by a small racing newspaper.

It was in 1977 that Mark got serious about asphalt racing. The team built a Camaro, which they painted bright orange. It had a white roof and a black hood. This car was designed just for racing on asphalt. Mark was a senior in high school by this time, and although he raced frequently, his dad made sure that Mark wouldn't miss school. Mark's love for racing had grown even more over the years. He did not even attend his high school graduation. He was out racing. That night he broke the Springfield, Missouri, track record.

Once he graduated, Mark took a job at the auto shop owned by fellow driver Larry Phillips. He worked for Larry, building parts and welding and fabricating sheet metal panels for the cars. And every weekend he raced, competing against some of the best drivers around.

ON HIS WAY

B y 1977, Mark had moved to racing in the American Speed Association (ASA) series, where the best short-track drivers in the Midwest competed. In this series, Mark was competing against some of the best drivers in the region and doing well. The big race of that year was the National Short Track Championship in Rockford, Illinois. The last thing Mark expected was to win the race, but he did. He spent the first half of the race in third place behind two top-notch drivers, but when one crashed and the other had mechanical problems, Mark became the leader. He won the race, finishing three seconds ahead of the second driver. At the end of the year, Mark was named Rookie of the Year.

It was Mark's best year of racing so far, but along with the thrills of success came the reality that racing cost a lot of money. Mark and his dad began looking for a sponsor. They hoped that the newspaper articles and other recognition Mark had

Racers at the start of the Dura-Lube/Big Kmart 400 race at North Carolina Motor Speedway in February, 1999. On his way to another successful season, Mark Martin won the race.

received would convince a company to back them financially.

Getting a sponsor for the team, however, was almost impossible. Instead, the team ended up working with manufacturers to get their products for free, in exchange for putting the company name on their car. Like most other drivers, Mark received all kinds of free parts for his car, including tires and engines.

One of the people who sponsored the team in this way was a car builder named Ed Howe, who had advised the team on setting the car up for asphalt racing. He had been critical of the team's initial work, mainly because the car weighed too much and therefore wouldn't be very fast. After making many changes, Mark had a car that was fast—so fast that it caught Ed's attention. For the 1978 season Ed offered Mark a free chassis, the supporting structure of the vehicle.

The team took the chassis and spent the winter preparing the new car. Although Mark was 19 years old, he was still short and very thin. The seat had to be moved so he could see over the steering wheel and reach the foot pedals. Once racing started that year, the team was spending more time on the road on the way to races than Mark was on the track. Instead of the three-hour drives they were used to, they now sometimes drove 14 hours to get to a race track. It was hard on everyone.

Mark's dad Julian said, "A typical weekend was Springfield [Missouri] on Friday night, and a little speedway up near Janesville, Wisconsin, on Saturday night, a little town over in Michigan on Sunday afternoon and then sometimes back to Toledo, Ohio, on Sunday night. And then we'd be back home on Monday to go to work."

Traveling from Arkansas to races all over the Midwest was not easy, but it did not seem to affect Mark's or the crew's performance. In 1978, Mark was leading the season in points, but he had yet to win a race. That was about to change.

Mark was driving in the Redbud 300, a 300-lap race on a quarter-mile long asphalt oval, at the Anderson Speedway in Indiana. It was the 15th race of the season. Mark had been following closely behind the leader, a driver named Dick Trickle, when he realized that his car's handling was getting worse. At lap 250, Mark noticed Dick pointing to his tire—it was going flat. Mark needed to pull into the pits to have the tire changed, but if he did he would run the risk of losing a lap and the chance of winning the race. If his tire went flat before the race was over, all would be lost anyway. Julian decided that Mark should come into the pits.

During a caution flag, when the drivers on the track must maintain their current positions and drive at a slower speed, the team saw their opportunity and Mark came in for a pit stop. They sprang into action, moving as quickly as they could to change the tire. Mark left the pit area less than 14 seconds later—an incredible speed for a pit stop. Mark had not lost a lap. In fact, he was in third place behind Dick, who was still leading, and another driver named Mike Eddy.

When the green flag came out to signal the start of the race again, Mark drove past Mike.

For 25 laps, Mark tried to get past Dick and take the lead. He finally succeeded on lap 286 and led the race until he crossed the finish line. At the end Mark said, "My crew won the race for me. I couldn't believe how fast they got me out."

Fast pit stops were a key part of the team's strategy and a big part of what made Mark lead in the races the majority of the time. With each race Mark became a better driver, and the crew learned something else about preparing his car or servicing it during the pit stops. In fact the team was doing so well that Mark stayed the points leader for the rest of 1978, and went on to win the ASA championship. He was 19 years old and a champion driver. Mark's future looked bright, but that also meant that everyone expected him to win—his family, the crew, his fans, and even himself.

Everyone felt the pressure and soon tension began to build between the team members. Mark decided it would be best to be out on his own. He made a deal with a man named Ray Dillon for a free trailer, and by the time their conversation was over, many things had changed. Ray had convinced Mark to move to Indiana, where his shop was. He offered Mark a shop to work on his car and a house on his property that he would rent to Mark for very little money. Mark accepted the offer. He and some of his crew members took all the racing equipment and moved to North Liberty, Indiana.

When they arrived in Indiana, they soon discovered that things weren't quite the way they had pictured. The shop did not have any heat or insulation. It was cold and so drafty that snow sometimes blew in around the door and

windows. Although the offer was not as good as it sounded, Mark was still happy. There were no more 12-hour drives to get to the ASA races. Mark's dad, Julian, continued to help out and came to almost all of the races.

During the 1979 season, Mark raced well again, winning the championship for the second year in a row. The team worked hard, sometimes 18-hour days, on every aspect of Mark's race car. Right before the qualifying laps of a race, the crew waxed the car and sprayed the underside, as well as the tires and wheels,

Mark Martin credits the speedy work of his pit crews, like the one pictured here at the Miller Lite 400 in 1998, for helping him to win many of his races.

with silicone. This reduced the wind resistance on the car and made Mark go faster.

Although being the champion for the second straight year was memorable, there was another reason why this year was important. Ray Dillon had been working on a modified version of the chassis that Mark currently drove. Ray experimented by trying several new things, hoping that Mark would be able to drive even faster on the track. The experimental car was ready in the summer, and Mark competed with the car, named the Mark II, at a race in Michigan.

Mark did well in the race with the new car, but it was clear they still had a lot to do. Mark and Ray worked on the new chassis together, making even more improvements. After some more experimenting and a change in tire manufacturers, Mark won his first race with the new Mark II chassis. In the three races that followed, he came in second every time.

Once the other teams began to see how terrific the new car was, they started asking Ray to build them one too. Soon Ray made a conversion kit so people could change the cars they already owned to the new system. The new Mark II car was a huge success.

Mark had his share of hard times in 1980 as well. He had a serious accident on the track early in the summer, breaking his right ankle and left leg and foot. Since Mark could not drive for about a month, he hired Darrell Waltrip to drive his car for him. (Darrell later won three Winston Cup series and Mark races against him today.) Before this race, Mark told Darrell that he wanted his car to start the race first and to win. Darrell had to work hard during the race, struggling against some of the top

drivers and also getting comfortable within the car, which was designed for Mark's small size, not Darrell's bigger body. But Darrell won anyway, making both him and Mark very happy.

Mark raced the rest of the year, winning several races and breaking some track records. Winning the championship that year was very important to Mark because he knew that it was again time to move toward his dream of racing on the NASCAR circuit.

NASCAR driver Darrell Waltrip, who once drove Mark Martin's car to victory when Martin couldn't race because of injuries.

THE LEARNING CURVE

Mark was 22 years old when he ran in his first Winston Cup race. It was at North Wilkesboro Speedway on April 3, 1981. Mark drove a new car that he, along with Ray Dillon, the car's owner, and the crew, had built over the previous winter. Mark had decided to race in just a few Winston Cup events that year and also compete in several other racing series. During that winter the team also built four other cars to race in different events, including the ASA series. One car was raced in the NASCAR's Busch Grand National (formerly the Sportsman) class.

In Mark's first Winston Cup race at North Wilkesboro, he qualified in fifth place. He did not finish in this race, only completing 166 laps before he had mechanical problems that forced him to leave the track. In his nervousness at the start of the race, Mark had forgotten to turn on the pump that cooled the rear end. Mark had never had this

During the early '80s, Mark Martin's racing career faced a number of challenges. It took a lot of sweat and hard work to overcome this difficult period of his life.

pump in his previous race cars, and he had not paid attention to it. By lap 166 a cylinder in Mark's engine was not operating, and the rear end was smoking because it was so hot.

Mark's second Winston Cup race was in Nashville. In qualifying, Mark did well, finishing sixth, but during practice he had more engine trouble. The entire crew, including Mark, worked fast to replace the problem engine with a new one. However, as the race wore on, Mark's car had additional mechanical problems and he finished last.

Discouraged but determined to do better, he spent two months making changes to his car. Mark knew that his car was not set up right for Winston Cup racing, but he did not know exactly what he needed to change to make it better. Mark did some experimenting and when he returned to Nashville for his third Winston Cup race, he had the best qualifying time and won the pole position.

Winning this position meant that Mark would be the first driver in line when the race started. The driver who won the pole also received money for starting first. Racing is a very expensive sport, especially Winston Cup racing. Mark was racing in several series, and that meant he needed a lot of money to pay his crew and to pay for parts to keep his cars in good working condition. The money from winning the pole helped Mark to meet some of his racing expenses.

It was very hot in Nashville on the night of Mark's third Winston Cup race, which meant that it would be really hard on the drivers and their cars. Any long race is a strain on the drivers both mentally, from needing to

concentrate so hard for so long, and physically, from driving at high speeds in close quarters. Mark did not know exactly how to prepare for this 420 lap race when it was so hot. He would soon learn what a strain it would be on his car and himself.

Mark started out well, leading for the first 36 laps. Quickly, though, his car began to show signs of wear. His tires felt as if they were worn and the car was not handling well at all. In addition Mark had not adjusted his seat properly, and as the race wore on it became harder and harder to reach the pedals.

He said, "I was a lap down before the first caution and after another sixty laps I got lapped again. I finally finished eleventh. I was

Problems with his cars, troubles with his crews, and frequent accidents plagued Mark Martin during his early years on the Winston Cup circuit. Above, Mark's car (no. 60) is being ridden up against the outside wall by another driver.

five laps down. It was the most humiliating defeat I'd ever had." Darrell Waltrip, who had raced Mark's car in an ASA race the year before, was one of the drivers competing at Nashville. Darrell won the race.

Mark did not compete in a Winston Cup race again until the middle of September. In between his third and fourth races, he took the car back to the shop in Indiana and made more changes. He had let a driver named Morgan Shepherd race the car at Michigan, and Morgan crashed it. The crew fixed the car and headed to Richmond for their fourth Winston Cup race. Mark won the pole position again. But again the team made an error. This time a crew member had left a rag in the engine, which gave Mark trouble. He struggled and finished the race seventh.

The Old Dominion 500 at the Martinsville Speedway was Mark's last Winston Cup race for the year. This time he qualified fifth, but when the race started, his car performed well and even led in some laps. He finished the race third. To Mark, he was well on his way to becoming a successful NASCAR driver.

Although Mark had only entered five Winston Cup races and spent most of his time on the track competing in other race series, Mark wanted to race in the Winston Cup series full-time the next season. In fact, Mark not only wanted to compete in the Winston Cup races in 1982, he was determined to win the Rookie of the Year title.

The first thing Mark did was talk to Ray Dillon. However, Ray did not want to move from Indiana to North Carolina, where the team found it easier to race on the Winston

Cup circuit. So Mark and a few people from the race shop began building a Winston Cup car on their own time. Soon he moved to North Carolina and his mom, Jackie, became his business manager.

Mark needed a sponsor to pay for the costs of racing a Winston Cup car for an entire season. The top teams were getting around $300,000 per racing season. The Apache Stove company agreed to sponsor Mark, but he was only able to get them to agree to $50,000 for the season. It was not a lot, but Mark decided it was better than nothing and agreed.

Everything was a struggle for Mark and the team in 1982. First he had to fire his crew chief early in the season. Then the Apache Stove Company never gave him the sponsorship money they had agreed on. The car consistently ran poorly. The truck that hauled Mark's car had an accident. The crew made mistakes. Mark's dream of winning the Rookie of the Year title would never be a reality. Although he had been the favorite to win the title, he lost it to another driver named Geoff Bodine.

The team was a mess and Mark had no money to pay the bills. His dad, Julian, did not have enough money to help him. To cover part of what he owed, Mark made one of his cars available, with Julian driving, to the people who were filming the movie *Stroker Ace* with Burt Reynolds. It was one way to make some money.

With everything in disarray, Mark decided that he wanted to drive for someone else instead of owning his own team. Soon a team owner named J. D. Stacy asked Mark to drive his car. Mark started the 1983 season racing for J. D., but he still had problems. To pay off more of his debts, Mark held an auction and sold all of his race equipment.

During the race at the Martinsville Speedway that year, Mark bumped Dale Earnhardt, causing him to spin. It was the same place where, two years before, Mark had placed third in his fifth Winston Cup race. This time he was fired at the end of the race. Mark had not won for seven races, and the owner did not want to wait any longer.

Finding a new owner who needed a driver was not easy. Mark drove a few races with several different teams and finally ended up with a team named Morgan-McClure Racing. The team was only racing a partial schedule, so Mark only drove in six more races. At the end of the season, he knew he did not want to continue with them. Mark thought his career was over.

Racing was Mark's entire life. For years, he had not done anything except live for racing. If he was not working on the car or helping with it, he was managing his team or studying the other drivers to improve his own driving. Day and night, everything he did revolved around the sport. When it seemed as if there were no hope for a career as a Winston Cup driver, Mark began drinking. He never liked alcohol. He had always stayed away from it because it scared him to see his father drunk. When he was with the crew and other drivers, he would often get teased because he would order a beer and then only take a few sips of it.

"I went from drinking so little I couldn't even keep from being teased about it, to where I almost even enjoyed it a little bit, to having some fun once in awhile, like a normal drinker

At the end of the 1983 season, Mark Martin turned to alcohol when he believed his career as a Winston Cup driver was over.

does, to drinking in excess. Alcoholism is like a disease that grows to maturity. You get to a certain point where you can't control it," Mark said. It would be several years before he conquered his alcohol problem.

This was probably the lowest point of Mark's life. His determined spirit, which had once helped him climb into a race car before he was old enough to have a driver's license, was gone.

LOOKING UP

Mark's racing career was in big trouble. He had lost all of his sponsors, both those who supported him financially and many of those who gave him racing parts. He had no money of his own to invest in his racing. Julian, Mark's dad, came to his rescue and bought him two race cars. Then Mark began working with an engine builder named Ron Neal. They had worked together when Mark raced in the ASA series. Ron suggested that they pair up and build a Ford for Mark to drive in the next ASA series.

At the time Ford was just beginning to support racing again, but no one was racing a Ford at the short tracks. No one thought a Ford could be competitive. Ron, however, thought differently and went to meet Lee Morse, a man who worked in Ford's racing division. Lee helped the new team get started by supplying them with parts, while Ron built the engines.

Mark Martin, his wife Arlene, and their son Matt, share a moment together after Mark has won another race.

41

At the same time that Mark was figuring out what do with his racing career, his sister Glenda introduced him to her friend, Arlene. Mark was 24 years old and felt that he was ready to settle down. Arlene was nearly 30 years old, divorced, and had four children. Although Arlene initially did not fit Mark's idea of his "dream girl," he liked her immediately.

Arlene, on the other hand, was not eager to get to know Mark. She was not really interested in dating anyone, and she was not at all interested in racing. But when she and Mark met, she liked him too. She thought he was nice and liked talking to him. Mark and Arlene became friends. They spent a lot of time talking, but Arlene made it clear she did not want to date.

When Mark returned from visiting his family and Arlene in Arkansas, he met and made a deal with Randy Rieble, a race car owner who lived in Wisconsin. Mark was to drive Randy's car in the 1984 ASA series. Mark moved to Wisconsin so he could work with his new team in Randy's shop.

He went back to Arkansas in January 1984 for his sister's birthday and went to see Arlene. By this time the two had spent many hours talking on the telephone and becoming even closer friends. Mark had decided to drive to Florida for the Daytona 500, in the hopes that he would find someone who needed a driver. He asked Arlene to go with him.

The Daytona 500 was the first race that Arlene had ever been to, and for Mark, it was one of the rare occasions when he was just a spectator. Mark did not find anyone who needed a driver and, although it was depressing not to be out on the track, he tried to concentrate on the good things he had and remind himself that he would get there again someday. On the ride home he told Arlene that he wanted to marry her, and later in the spring, the two got engaged. They were married on October 27, 1984.

The 1984 racing season was the hardest season ever for Mark. In the time he had been gone, the series had changed. The cars were different. Mark and the team struggled to get everything set up. By the end of the season, Mark had won just one race and one pole in the series. It was a big change from winning the ASA Championship in 1980 for the second year in a row.

At the end of the year, Mark received an offer to drive for another team. He said yes and joined forces with Benny Ertel and Jim Fennig. This was the beginning of a long partnership between the three. Today Benny is Mark's business manager and Jim is the crew chief for the team. Joining the new team, which was owned by Jerry Gunderman, was just what Mark needed.

In Mark's first year with the team, things started to get brighter. He won four races and six pole positions, placing fourth in points for the year. The following year he was once again the ASA Champion. After winning with the Ford, Mark was again considered a pioneer in racing, just as he was when he raced with the Mark II chassis. In 1986 Mark was also working his way back into Winston Cup racing. He raced five times in the series for his team owner but did not do very well.

In 1987 he made a step toward Winston Cup

Jack Roush, the owner of Roush Racing, inspects a racing Ford's sparkplugs. In 1987 he wanted to get involved in the Winston Cup series and chose Mark Martin as a driver for his new team. Mark still races for Roush today.

racing when he moved to the Busch Grand National series. In order to race a full season in this series he moved his family to Greensboro, North Carolina. Mark drove a Ford with a V-8 engine, owned by Bruce Lawmaster, in this series, which was just one step below Winston Cup. Although his car weighed a lot more than the Chevys and Buicks with V-6 engines that were most often used in this series, Mark did well. In May he won at Dover, marking the first time that a Ford had won in the series.

Toward the end of the season, Mark had an important meeting with Jack Roush. Jack was a former racer who owned a big automotive company. He was the owner of several racing teams, but now he wanted to get involved in the Winston Cup series. Jack had been an engineer at Ford Motor Company for many years, so his connections with Ford were very good.

Steve Hmiel and Robin Pemberton became crew chiefs and were given the job of getting Jack's team going. Jack considered several drivers for his new team, but in the end he chose Mark. "Mark was the only one who was more interested in who was going to work on the car and what kind of cars they were going to be and how much money we were going to spend on testing, rather than how much money he was going to make," Jack commented.

Mark eagerly took the job as the driver on Jack's new team. Although Roush Racing has grown tremendously since that first year, Mark continues to race for Jack today. Steve Hmiel is still working on the team and is currently the general manager at Roush Racing.

The team's first season in 1988 was difficult. Although Mark finished second at Bristol and won a pole position at Dover, that was the extent of his success. When it was over, Mark ended up placing only 15th for the year—one position lower than when he tried his first full season of Winston Cup racing.

In 1989 things started to turn around for Mark and the Roush Racing team. Mark was running well, finishing second several times and sitting on the pole often. Then, on October 22, 1989, Mark won his first Winston Cup race. It was also the first victory for Roush Racing and one of the greatest moments of Mark's life. On Victory Lane he said, "My life is fulfilled. I feel like I'm the luckiest man alive."

In 1990 Mark performed even better on the race track. In fact it was the first of many terrific seasons of Winston Cup racing for Mark. Just the same, it held one of Mark's biggest disappointments. At Richmond, early in the season, Mark won the race when he opted to take two tires instead of four in the last pit stop. He was the first one out of the pits and as a result won the race over Dale Earnhardt.

But when the NASCAR officials inspected his car after the race, they found a problem. The officials said that a carburetor spacer was thicker than the rules allowed. The officials fined the team $40,000, and although they let him keep his win, they took away 46 of the points he won. The ruling upset the team, who knew that the problem could have been solved by simply welding the spacer into position. Also the car had been through several inspections earlier in the weekend, and no one had said it was a problem. It was a great disappointment, but it would not be clear how much it meant until the end of the season.

As the racing season continued, Mark persevered and became a top contender. Before long he was leading in points for the year. It looked like he had a real chance at winning the championship. Race after race two drivers fought for the championship—Mark Martin and Dale Earnhardt. It all came down to the last race, and Mark lost the championship to Dale. The difference between first and second place was just 26 points.

At the end of the season, the one thing that everyone seemed to remember was the race earlier that year at Richmond and the 46 points Mark had lost. It seemed unfortunate that the

NASCAR officials had penalized Mark's team when their carburetor set-up didn't give them any mechanical advantage over anyone else. If that one thing had been different, Mark would have won the championship.

But Mark chose not to look back. Instead, he said that since he was third the year before and second that year, that the next year, 1991, he planned to finish first.

Mark Martin celebrates a victory with his crew. 1990 was the beginning of many successful seasons of Winston Cup racing for Martin and his team.

WINSTON CUP STAR

In 1991 Mark did not have the championship year he had hoped for, with the team placing sixth in points at the end of the year. Just the same, he had become one of the top drivers on the circuit—a force that challenged every driver at every race. In fact Mark's skills as a driver, combined with a top-notch team, have since placed him among the top six drivers in Winston Cup racing since 1989.

Mark claimed just one Winston Cup victory in 1991, in the last race of the season. He had so many troubles that year that he couldn't quite believe that he won. At Talladega earlier in the year, Mark got caught in the middle when Ernie Irvan bumped Kyle Petty, causing Petty to spin. Mark was sent on a wild ride when his car started spinning too. The rear end lifted up in the air so high that it was nearly standing on its nose. Incredibly the car landed on its wheels and Mark was not hurt. He actually completed the race, taking 24th place.

Mark Martin flashes a broad smile as he displays his trophy, while his son Matt, who often attends races with his father, gives a big thumbs up for his dad's Winston Cup star performance.

Mark Martin (right) confers with his crew chief, Jimmy Fennig. Good communications between the driver and the crew chief are critical for any team to succeed. Mark is always quick to acknowledge his crew chief and team whenever he wins a race.

Much of the year was filled with mechanical problems. Later in the season, Mark had won the pole in Charlotte and then led for much of the race. It looked like he might be able to win, and Mark feared it was too good to be true. He was right. He finished 35th after his engine developed serious problems.

As the 1991 season came to an end, Mark and the team had to say goodbye to one of the crew. Robin Pemberton, who had been with the team since it began with Jack Roush, left to become Kyle Petty's crew chief. It was decided that Steve Hmiel would take over Robin's position. In addition, Mark's sponsor, Folger's Coffee, had decided to end their financial backing. At the last race of 1991, Mark announced that Valvoline would take over sponsorship the next year.

Although the race year was not as successful as the team had hoped, there was still one reason that 1991 was memorable for Mark. On December 17 his son, Matthew Clyde, was born. Growing up with a Winston Cup star driver for a father is pretty interesting. Matt often attends races and can sometimes be seen hanging out with his dad by the transporter. When he was five years old, Matt put on his helmet and tested out a go-kart for the first time. Although Mark had learned how to drive when he was very young, he still thought watching Matt on the track was "kind of scary."

In 1992 Mark found himself in a race for the championship with five other drivers. Again he had struggled through the spring and summer, almost always placing in the top ten, but not winning a race. After winning the Mello Yello 500 and realizing that he had a chance at the championship, Mark was cautious. He told reporters, "We raced to win [at the Mello Yello 500] and we'll race to win at Rockingham. We won't race for points. We'll win the championship if it's meant to be." The team learned quickly that it wasn't meant to be when Mark had an accident at Rockingham and finished 30th. Mark ended the season in sixth place.

The 1993 and 1994 racing seasons were two

of the saddest years in Winston Cup racing. In 1993 driver Alan Kulwicki died in a plane crash, and Davey Allison perished in a helicopter accident. In the first hours of practice for the first race of 1994, the Daytona 500, Neil Bonnett was killed when he lost control of his car. A few days later, Rodney Orr was also killed in an accident on the track.

Other changes in the world of Winston Cup racing took place in 1993. Teams had really begun to look at the aerodynamics of their cars, trying to figure out ways to reduce wind resistance. Teams also wanted to increase the downforce to the car, which would make it stick to the track better. Mark went to his team with an idea; he asked them to build a car with the nose lower and the roof at the minimum height. The team didn't think it would work, but they built the car anyway. It was much faster, and Mark placed third in points at the end of the year.

Everyone in NASCAR was saddened by the deaths of Neil and Rodney in the beginning of 1994, but the racing still went on. Then at Talladega, Mark was involved in a serious crash. Caught again in the middle of an accident, Mark lost his brakes and went sailing off the track at full speed. An in-car camera showed the view from Mark's car, which headed straight into a guardrail and through two chain link fences, finally stopping when it hit another guardrail, right near some fans. It was a scary ride for Mark, but miraculously he emerged only slightly bruised.

In Michigan there was another devastating wreck. Ernie Irvan crashed into the wall during practice and was critically injured. Mark, who

was friends with Ernie, was in shock. A week later, he drove Ernie's car in the Busch Grand National race at Bristol. "I want to make sure this team can be an asset to the family and to keep it in good standing," Mark said. It took a long time, but Ernie recovered and returned to Winston Cup racing. Mark was third again in points for the year.

Chevys and the Fords have characteristically been in competition with each other in

Mark Martin appreciates every trip onto Victory Lane. "Every time I win, I know that could be my last one . . . ever," he says.

During the 1996 season Mark Martin had a lot to smile about. He had six victories in the Busch Grand National series and won his second IROC championship.

stock car racing. Frequently one or the other stands out during the race season. In 1995, it was the Chevy Monte Carlos. Mark won four of just eight victories that the Ford Thunderbirds saw that year. At the end of the season, he was fourth in points but was the highest ranked Ford driver. It was a good feeling.

The 1996 season had its up and downs for Mark. He didn't have any victories in the Winston Cup series, but he won six times in the Busch Grand National series and logged his second IROC championship. He broke his streak of no wins in a big way by winning two races in a row in 1997, one at Sears Point and one at Dover. Steve, Mark's crew chief, had moved on to become the general manager at Roush Racing, and Mark was joined once again by his former ASA crew chief Jimmy Fennig. Many people felt that Jimmy brought some extra magic to the team because Mark and he worked so well together. The pair was completely in sync, understanding exactly what the car needed to allow Mark to push it to its fullest potential.

By the end of 1997, Jeff Gordon was almost guaranteed the championship unless something serious happened during the race at Atlanta. All Jeff needed to do was finish in 18th place or higher and he would win the championship. It was a tight race, however, between Mark and Dale Jarrett for second place. Although Mark ended up in third, he was considered a favorite for the championship when the 1998 season started.

However 1998 was not destined to be Mark's year for the championship. He worked hard, beginning with an almost entirely new crew, except for Jimmy, his crew chief, and Dennis Ritchie, his truck driver. The team gave champion Jeff Gordon a run for the title, but they just couldn't quite pull it off. Mark spent much of the season in constant pain from a herniated disc in his back, a problem which had bothered him since he was a teenager.

Sometimes it got so bad that he was unable to do simple things like put on his shoes. He finally found help from an acupuncturist who was able to relieve his pain. With all of his physical pain, and his emotional distress from loosing his family members in the plane crash, Mark still drove in every race that year, giving it his best shot.

In January 1999, the National Motorsports Press Association (NMPA) gave Mark the 1998 NMPA/Pocono Spirit Award in recognition of his sportsmanship, determination, and extra-ordinary performance in the face of adversity. The next month, Mark won his first victory of the season at Rockingham. Typically, it takes the team a few races to get going, so a win early in the season was particularly up-lifting. After 25 years of racing, Mark has learned to appreciate it each time he rolls onto Victory Lane. He said, "I know now that every time I win, I know that could be my last one that I ever win, ever."

CHRONOLOGY

1959   Born Mark Martin on January 9 to Julian and Jackie Martin in Batesville, Arkansas.

1974   Competes in his first stock car race on April 12 and wins the Arkansas Six-Cylinder championship in September.

1977   Named Rookie of the Year in the American Speed Association (ASA) series.

1978   Wins the ASA championship.

1979   Wins the ASA championship for the second year; begins to race with Ray Dillon's Mark II experimental chassis.

1981   Competes in his first Winston Cup race in April.

1982   Competes again in the Winston Cup series and performs poorly.

1983   Drives for another team in the Winston Cup races; begins to have drinking problem.

1984   Returns to compete in the ASA series after unsuccessful attempts at the Winston Cup series; marries sister's friend, Arlene.

1985   Again wins the ASA championship.

1988   Returns to Winston Cup series; drives for Jack Roush's new team.

1989   Wins first Winston Cup race in October and places third for the year.

1990   Second in points in Winston Cup competition for the year, only 26 points behind winner Dale Earnhardt.

1991   Son, Matthew Clyde, is born in December; Valvoline becomes Mark's primary sponsor.

1992–1997   Continues to compete regularly and becomes a top Winston Cup driver.

1998   Wins his fourth International Race of Champions (IROC) title to become the first to win four IROC titles; places second in points for the Winston Cup racing season; father, stepmother, and stepsister die in a plane crash.

1999   Receives National Motorsports Press Association (NMPA) Pocono Spirit Award in January; wins his first Winston Cup race of the season at Rockingham in February.

STATISTICS

YEAR	RACES	WINS	TOP 5	TOP 10	WINNINGS
1981	5	0	1	2	$13,950
1982	30	0	2	8	126,655
1983	16	0	1	3	99,655
1984	0	0	0	0	0
1985	0	0	0	0	0
1986	5	0	0	0	20,515
1987	1	0	0	0	3,550
1988	29	0	3	10	223,630
1989	29	1	14	18	1,019,250
1990	29	3	16	23	1,302,958
1991	29	1	14	17	1,039,991
1992	29	2	10	17	1,000,571
1993	30	5	12	19	1,657,662
1994	31	2	15	20	1,628,906
1995	31	4	13	22	1,893,519
1996	31	0	14	23	1,887,396
1997	32	4	16	23	2,532,484
1998	33	7	22	26	3,524,720
CAREER	**390**	**29**	**153**	**231**	**$17,975,412**

FURTHER READING

Burt, Bill. *Behind The Scenes of NASCAR Racing.* Osceola: Motorbooks International, 1997.

Huff, Richard. *The Insider's Guide To Stock Car Racing.* Chicago: Bonus Books, 1997.

McGuire, Ann. *The History of NASCAR.* Philadelphia: Chelsea House Publishers, 2000.

Olney, Ross R. *How To Understand Auto Racing.* New York: Lothrop, Lee & Shepard Books, 1979.

Zeller, Bob. *Mark Martin, Driven to Race.* Phoenix: David Bull Publishing, 1997.

INDEX

ABOUT THE AUTHOR

Tara Baukus Mello is a freelance writer who specializes in the automotive industry. She has published over 1000 articles in newspapers and magazines. Baukus Mello is also the author of *Stunt Driving*, *Rusty Wallace*, and *The Pit Crew*, all part of the Race Car Legends series. A graduate of Harvard University, she lives in southern California where she cruises the streets in her 1932 Ford pickup street rod with her husband Jeff.